Fun & Jolly Christmas Songs

Arranged by Dan Coates

Alfred Music
P.O. Box 10003
Van Nuys, CA 91410-0003
alfred.com

ISBN-10: 0-7390-4403-6
ISBN-13: 978-0-7390-4403-2

(There's No Place Like)
Home for the Holidays

Words by
Al Stillman

Music by
Robert Allen
Arranged by Dan Coates

2

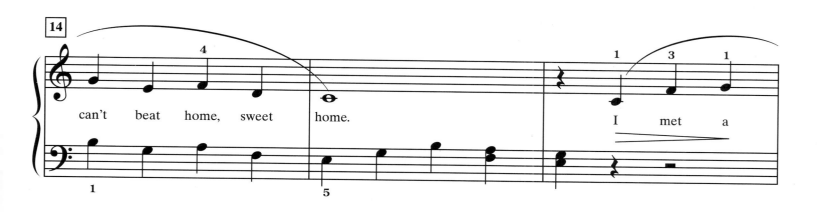

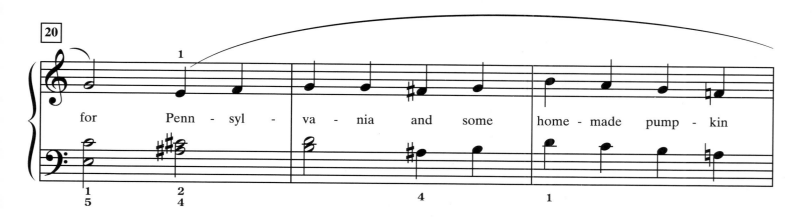

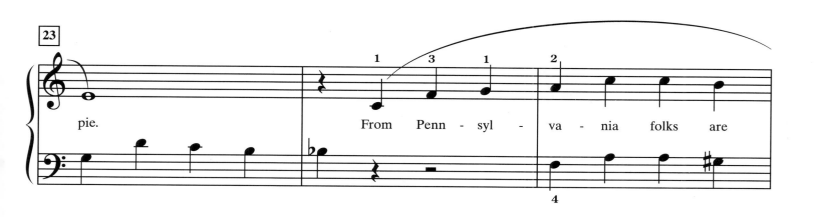

4

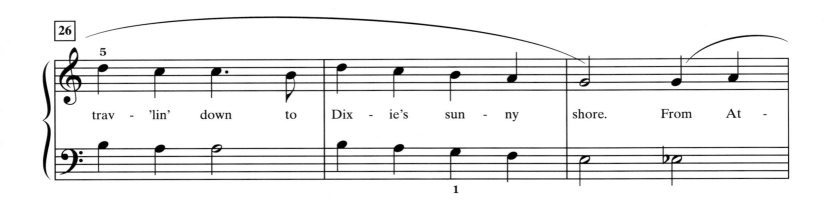

trav - 'lin' down to Dix - ie's sun - ny shore. From At -

D.S. 𝄋 al Coda

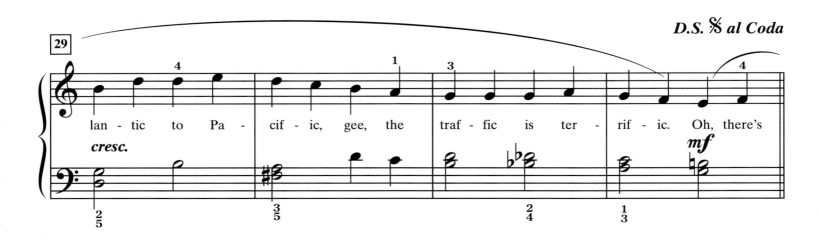

lan - tic to Pa - cif - ic, gee, the traf - fic is ter - rif - ic. Oh, there's

cresc.

mf

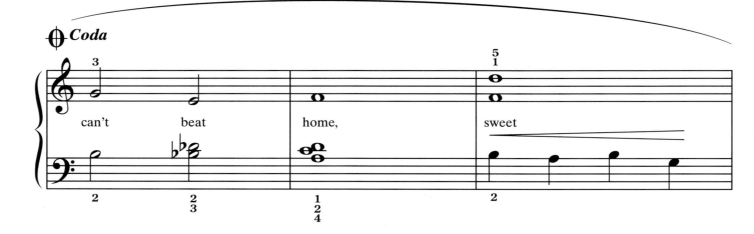

Coda

can't beat home, sweet

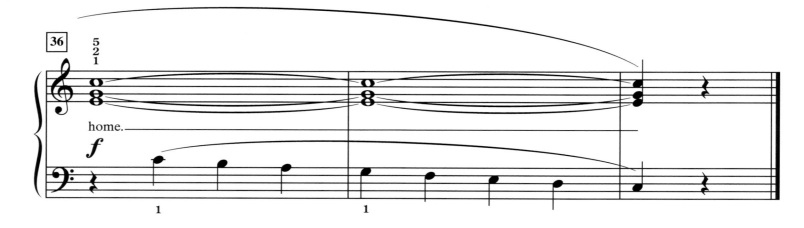

home.

f

Jingle Bell Rock

Words and Music by
Joe Beal and Jim Boothe
Arranged by Dan Coates

in the frost - y air. What a bright time.— It's the

right time—— to rock the night a - way. Jin - gle

bell time—— is a swell time—— to go glid - in' in a

one - horse sleigh. Gid - dy - up, jin - gle horse, pick up your feet.——

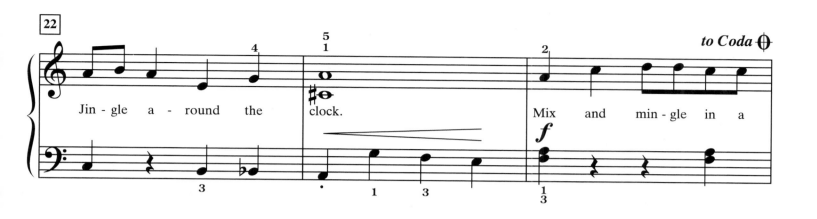

to Coda

Jin - gle a - round the clock. Mix and min - gle in a

D. S. al Coda

jin - gl - in' beat. That's the jin - gle bell rock.

Coda

jin - gl - in' beat. That's the jin - gle bell, that's the jin - gle bell,

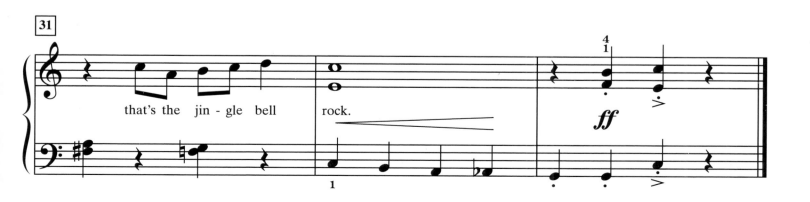

that's the jin - gle bell rock.

Toyland

Words by
Glen MacDonough

Music by
Victor Herbert
Arranged by Dan Coates

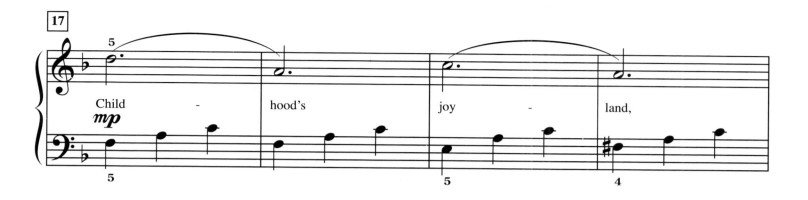

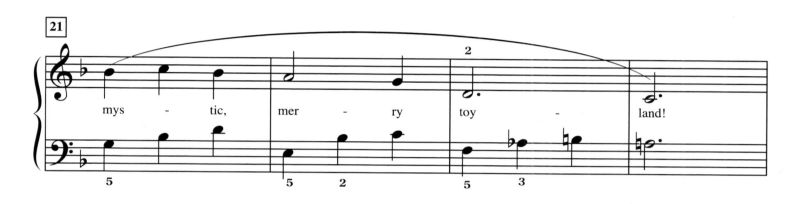

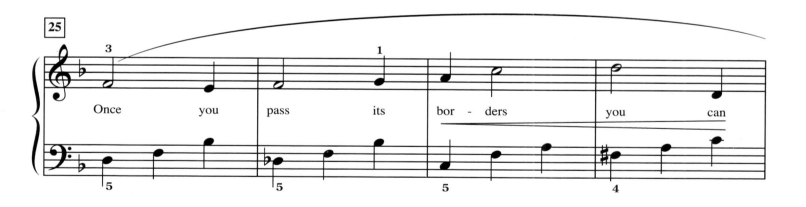

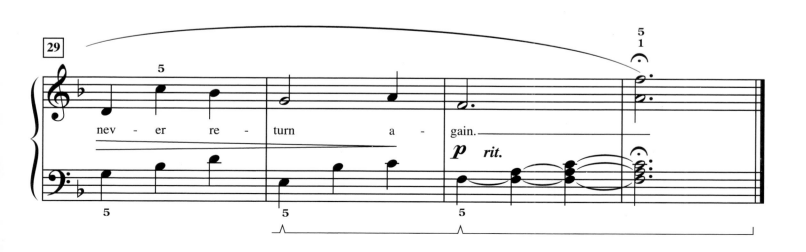

Winter Wonderland

Words by
Dick Smith

Music by
Felix Bernard
Arranged by Dan Coates

Jolly Old Saint Nicholas

Traditional
Arranged by Dan Coates

Nuttin' for Christmas

Words and Music by
Sid Teper and Roy C. Bennett
Arranged by Dan Coates

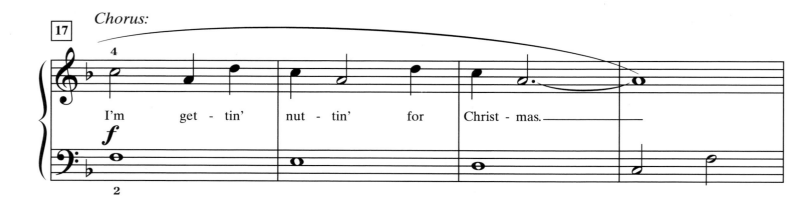

Chorus:

17 I'm get - tin' nut - tin' for Christ - mas.

f

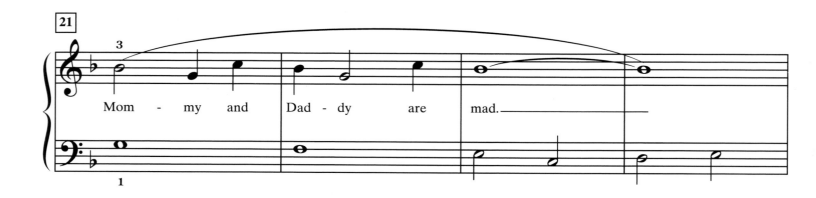

21 Mom - my and Dad - dy are mad.

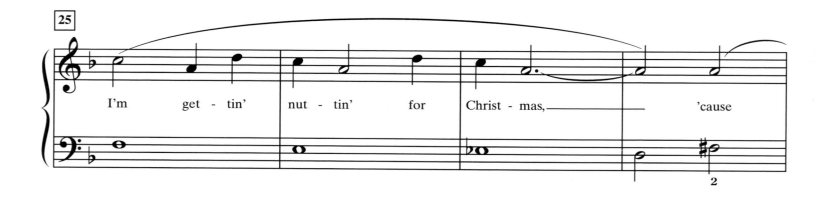

25 I'm get - tin' nut - tin' for Christ - mas, 'cause

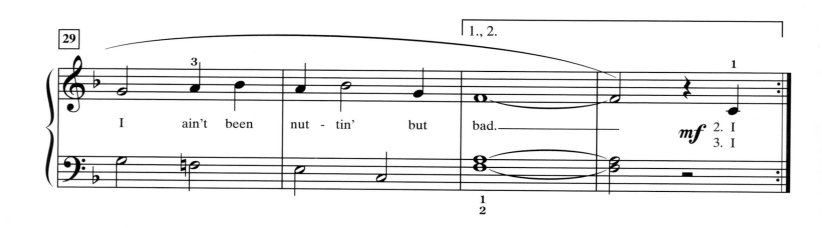

29 1., 2.

I ain't been nut - tin' but bad.

mf 2. I
3. I

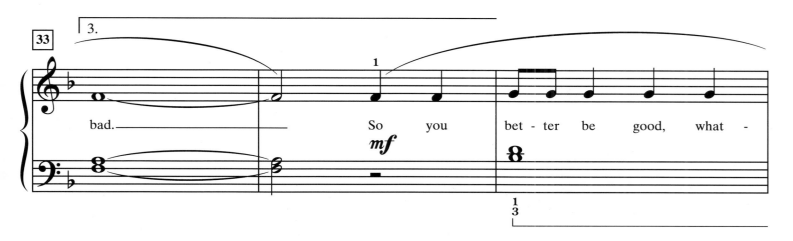

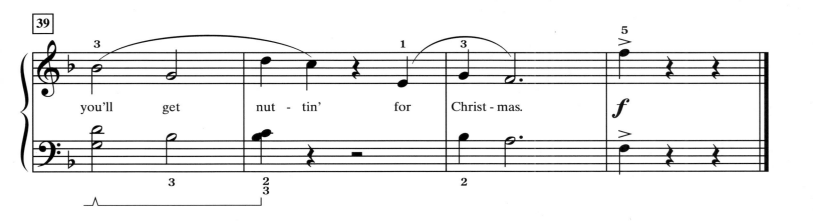

Verse 2:
I put a tack on teacher's chair;
Somebody snitched on me.
I tied a knot in Susie's hair;
Somebody snitched on me.
I did a dance on Mommy's plants,
Climbed a tree and tore my pants.
Filled the sugar bowl with ants;
Somebody snitched on me.
(To Chorus:)

Verse 3:
I won't be seeing Santa Claus;
Somebody snitched on me.
He won't come visit me because
Somebody snitched on me.
Next year I'll be going straight,
Next year I'll be good, just wait.
I'd start now but it's too late;
Somebody snitched on me.
(To Chorus:)

All I Want for Christmas Is My Two Front Teeth

Words and Music by
Don Gardner
Arranged by Dan Coates

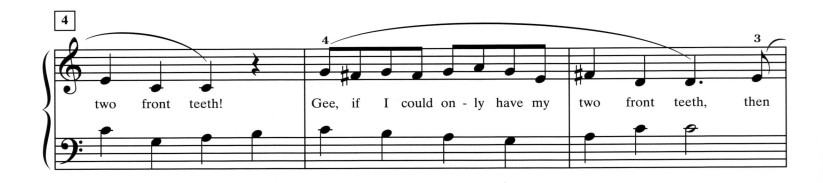

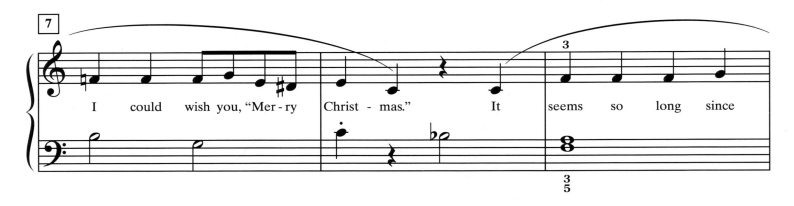

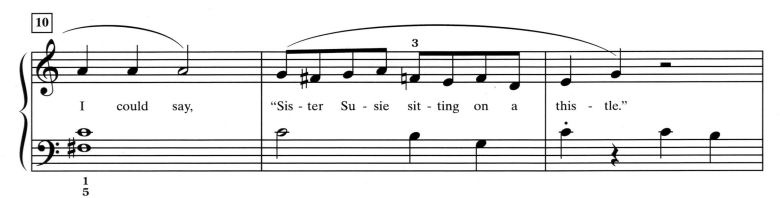

Ukrainian Bell Carol

Traditional
Arranged by Dan Coates

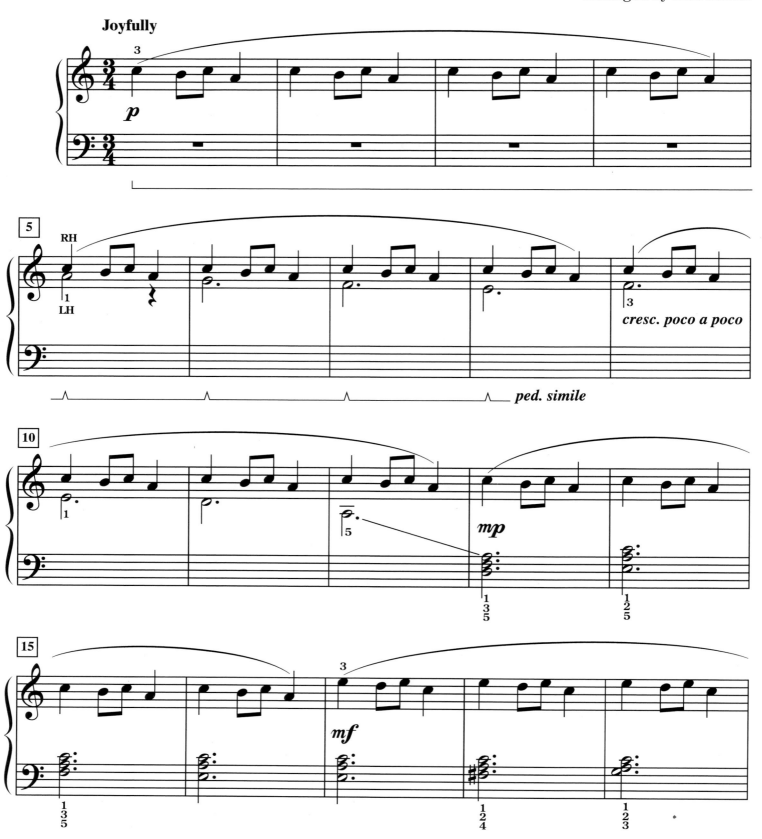

The Christmas Waltz

Words by
Sammy Cahn

Music by
Jule Styne
Arranged by Dan Coates

Have Yourself a Merry Little Christmas

Words and Music by
Hugh Martin and Ralph Blane
Arranged by Dan Coates

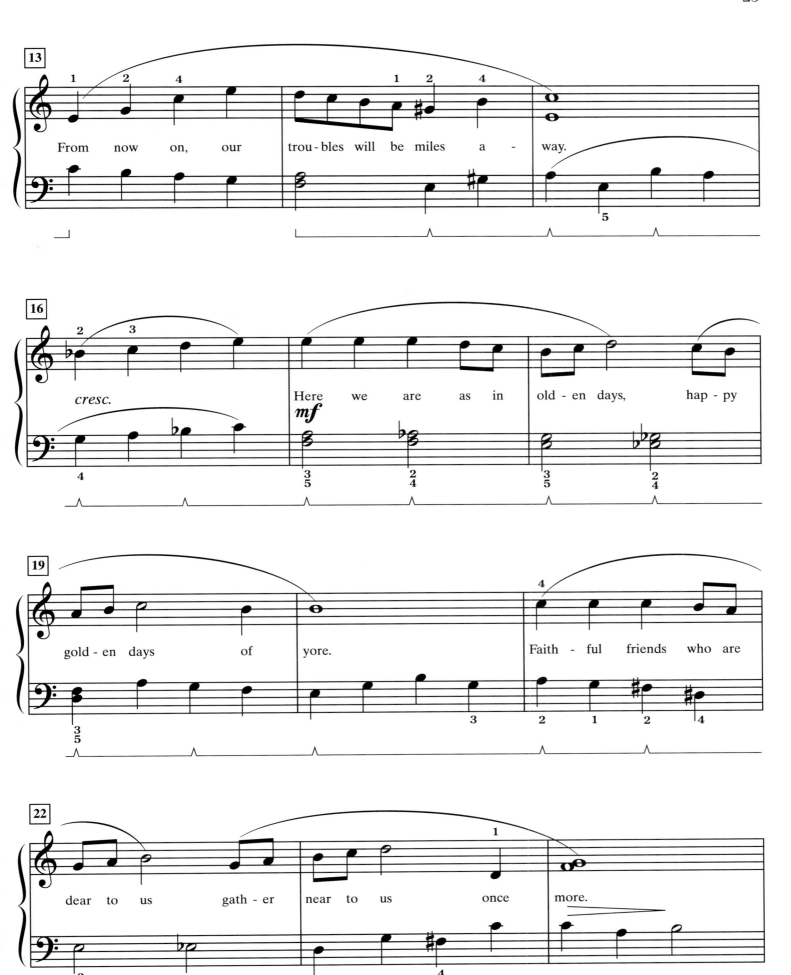